ESSENTIAL ELEMENTS
FOR STRINGS
A COMPREHENSIVE STRING METHOD

MICHAEL ALLEN • ROBERT GILLESPIE • PAMELA TELLEJOHN HAYES
ARRANGEMENTS BY JOHN HIGGINS

Congratulations for successfully completing Book 1 and welcome to Book 2 of *Essential Elements for Strings!* By now you are well aware of the benefits and joy of playing bass in the orchestra. The techniques you learned in Book 1 will help you reach a more advanced level in Book 2 that will make your musical experiences even more fun and exciting.

You can learn the new skills in the order they occur in Book 2, or you can master a particular skill at the time it most applies to your individual playing needs. Tabs appear on the sides of each page to help you quickly find the section or concept you need to practice.

There will be rewards for your effort! As you spend time learning more challenging material, the mastery of new skills will bring you even more joy in the years to come. Good luck, and best wishes for a lifetime of musical happiness!

To create an account, visit:
www.essentialelementsinteractive.com

Student Activation Code
"E2DB-6895-3298-1429"

ISBN 978-0-634-05268-2
Copyright © 2004 by HAL LEONARD CORPORATION
International Copyright Secured   All Rights Reserved

HAL•LEONARD®
CORPORATION
7777 W. BLUEMOUND RD. P.O. BOX 13819 MILWAUKEE, WI 53213

T0055347

REVIEW

KEY SIGNATURE	TIME SIGNATURE	NOTES			SLUR
Key of D	4/4	Whole	Half	Quarter	

Major Scale — A Major Scale is a series of eight notes that follow a definite pattern of whole steps and half steps. Half steps appear only between scale steps 3–4 and 7–8. Every major scale has the same arrangement of whole steps and half steps.

1. TUNING TRACK

2. D MAJOR SCALE – Round *(When group A reaches ②, group B begins at ①)*

3. D MAJOR ARPEGGIO

4. D MAJOR MANIA

Legato — Play in a smooth and connected style.

5. THEME FROM LONDON SYMPHONY

Franz J. Haydn (1732–1809)

REVIEW

TIME SIGNATURE	NOTES		TIE	TEMPO MARKING	1st & 2nd ENDINGS

Forte (*f*)   Piano (*p*)   Bow Lift (ʼ)

Dotted Half | **Eighths**

Moderato

6. D MAJOR IN THREES

III

Dynamics   crescendo (*cresc.*)   Gradually increase volume.
decrescendo (*decresc.*)   Gradually decrease volume.

7. DYNAMIC CONTRASTS

Norwegian composer **Edvard Grieg** wrote *Peer Gynt Suite* for a play by Henrik Ibsen in 1875, the year before the telephone was invented by Alexander Graham Bell. "Morning" is a melody from *Peer Gynt Suite*. Music used in plays, or in films and television, is called **incidental music**.

8. MORNING (from Peer Gynt)

Moderato

Edvard Grieg (1843–1907)

9. BARCAROLLE

Moderato

Jacques Offenbach (1819–1880)

WORKOUTS

Tunneling
Slide your fingers up and down the fingerboard between 2 strings.

Ridin' The Rails
Slide up and down one string with your fingers.

Tappin' And Slidin'
Tap your fingers on any string, slide toward the other end of the fingerboard, and tap again.

G MAJOR

REVIEW

KEY SIGNATURE

Key of G

HOOKED BOWING

TEMPO MARKING

Andante

10. G MAJOR SCALE – Round

11. G MAJOR ARPEGGIO

THEORY

Interval

The distance between two notes is called an interval. Start with "1" on the lower note, and count each line and space between the notes. The number of the higher note is the distance, or name, of the interval.

12. SCALE INTERVALS

2nd   3rd   4th   5th

6th   7th   8th or octave   *Name this interval.*

13. CHESTER

Andante

William Billings (1746–1800)

✔ Is your left hand shaped properly?

REVIEW

KEY SIGNATURE

Key of G *(Upper Octave – violin)*

TEMPO MARKING

Allegro

14. G MAJOR SCALE *(Upper Octave – violin)*

15. G MAJOR ARPEGGIO *(Upper Octave – violin)*

Intonation   Intonation is how well each note is played in tune.

16. INTONATION ENCOUNTER – Duet

17. THE OUTBACK

Allegro

REVIEW

KEY SIGNATURE **TIME SIGNATURE** **STACCATO**

Key of C

18. C MAJOR SCALE

19. C MAJOR ARPEGGIO

20. C MAJOR DUET

21. BUFFALO GALS

Allegretto ◁ *A lively tempo, faster than Andante, but slower than Allegro.*

Cool White (John Hodges)

✔ Check your bow hand. Are your fingers curved and is your thumb bent?

REVIEW

KEY SIGNATURE

Key of C *(Lower Octave – viola and cello)*

TIME SIGNATURE

𝄴

TONE PRODUCTION
- place bow between bridge and fingerboard
- bow straight
- proper weight

22. C MAJOR SCALE – Round *(Lower Octave – viola and cello)*

23. C MAJOR ARPEGGIO *(Lower Octave – viola and cello)*

24. C MAJOR MANIA

Dynamics mp *(mezzo piano)* Play moderately soft.
mf *(mezzo forte)* Play moderately loud.

p — *piano*
mp — *mezzo piano*
mf — *mezzo forte*
f — *forte*

25. CROSSROADS

Moderato

CHANGING BOW SPEED

Change the bow speed according to the length of the note. When you have a longer note value, the bow speed should be slower. If there is a dotted half note on a down bow and a quarter note on an up bow, the speed of the bow must change.

Example:

Slow
Bow ⟶ Fast
Bow

RHYTHMS

26. THE DOT ALWAYS COUNTS

Slow
Bow ⟶ Fast
Bow

27. ALOUETTE

Allegretto

French Folk Song

28. RIGAUDON

Moderato

Henry Purcell (1659–1695)

29. ESSENTIAL CREATIVITY – OH! SUSANNAH

Make up your own dynamics and write them in the music. Play the line and describe how the dynamics change the sound.

Allegretto

Stephen C. Foster (1826–1864)

Eighth Note & Eighth Rest

30. RHYTHM RAP
Shadow bow and count before playing.

31. EIGHTH NOTES ON THE BEAT

32. SHORT AND SWEET

33. RHYTHM RAP
Shadow bow and count before playing.

34. EIGHTH NOTES OFF THE BEAT

35. SUNNY DAY

36. ESSENTIAL ELEMENTS QUIZ – JESSE JAMES

Moderato

Folk Ballad from Missouri

RHYTHMS

Dotted Quarter & Eighth Notes

A **dot** adds half the value of the quarter note.

37. RHYTHM RAP

Shadow bow and count before playing.

38. THE DOT COUNTS

39. WATCH THE DOT

40. D MAJOR SEQUENCE

41. DOTS ON THE MOVE

Fermata   Hold the note (or rest) longer than normal.

42. D MAJOR BONANZA – Duet

43. A CAPITAL SHIP

Moderato

American Folk Song

44. ESSENTIAL CREATIVITY

Create your own rhythms by penciling in a dot and a flag to change any two quarter notes from ♩ ♩ *to* ♩. ♪

45. HOOKED ON DOTS

Ritardando   *ritard.* (or) *rit.* – Gradually slower

46. THEME FROM NEW WORLD SYMPHONY

Lento ◁ *Very slow tempo*

Antonin Dvořák (1841–1904)

rit.

47. ESSENTIAL ELEMENTS QUIZ – RONDEAU

Jean-Joseph Mouret (1682–1738)

Andantino ◁ *A tempo that is slightly quicker than* **Andante**.

♩. ♪

RHYTHMS

SHARP KEYS

Team Work

Great musicians give encouragement to their fellow performers. Violin, viola, and cello players will now learn a new challenging skill. The success of your orchestra depends on everyone's talent and patience. Play your best as members of these sections advance their musical technique.

Special Double Bass Exercise

Draw a note next to each printed note that will match the interval number shown. The note you draw can be higher or lower than the printed note. The first one is done for you.

2nd	5th	3rd	octave	4th	6th	7th
(Example)			(go lower only)		(go lower only)	(go lower only)

Listening Skills

Play what your teacher plays. Listen carefully.

48. LET'S READ "C#" (C-sharp) – Review

49. STAY SHARP

50. AT PIERROT'S DOOR

Andante

French Folk Song

51. HOT CROSS BUNS

Moderato

✔ Were your C#'s in tune?

HALF POSITION ON THE G STRING

G♯ is played with 1 finger on the G string in half position (1/2).

Listening Skills
Play what your teacher plays. Listen carefully.

52. LET'S READ "G♯" (G-sharp)

53. REACHING OUT

54. HIGHER AND HIGHER

½ ◄ *Play with 2 fingers in half position.*

Key Signature A MAJOR

THEORY

Play all F's as F♯ (F-sharp), C's as C♯ (C-sharp), and G's as G♯ (G-sharp).

55. A MAJOR SCALE

56. ESSENTIAL ELEMENTS QUIZ – A SONG FOR ANNE

Moderato

SHARP KEYS

Special Double Bass Exercise

While the violas and cellos are learning a new note, choose any one pitch on the staff and make up a rhythm exercise. Use each of the following notes and rests at least once (♩. ♩ ♩ ♪ – 𝄽 𝄾). Be sure to line up your notes and rests with the counting. After you finish, shadow bow the exercise.

1 & 2 & 3 & 4 &   1 & 2 & 3 & 4 &   1 & 2 & 3 & 4 &   1 & 2 & 3 & 4 &

Listening Skills   Play what your teacher plays. Listen carefully.

57. LET'S READ "F♯" (F-sharp) – Review

58. HIGH POINT

59. MAGNIFICENT MONTANA

60. D MAJOR SCALE – Round

HISTORY In the second half of the 1800s many composers tried to express the spirit of their own country by writing music with a distinct national flavor. Listen to and describe the music of Scandinavian and Spanish composers, and Russian composers such as Borodin, Tchaikovsky, and Rimsky-Korsakov. They often used folk songs and dance rhythms to convey their nationalism.

61. RUSSIAN FOLK TUNE

G# (G-SHARP) ON THE E STRING

G#
is played with 4 fingers on the E string in first position (I).

Listening Skills   Play what your teacher plays. Listen carefully.

62. LET'S READ "G#" (G-sharp)

63. A MAJOR SCALE

64. A MAJOR ARPEGGIO

65. THE FIG TREE

Allegretto

f decresc.

cresc. f p

Accent   ♩ or ♪   Emphasize the note. Add weight or increase the speed at the beginning of the bow stroke.

66. SITKA CITY

Russian Folk Song

Moderato

mf p

f

RHYTHMS

Sixteenth Notes

4 sixteenth notes = 1 beat
1 e & a   Each sixteenth note = 1/4 beat

1 e & a 2 e & a

A single sixteenth note has 2 flags on the stem.

67. RHYTHM RAP

Shadow bow and count before playing.

Count: **1** e & a **2** & **1** e & a **2** & **1** e & a **2** & **1** & **2** &

68. SIXTEENTH NOTE FANFARE

69. TECHNIQUE TRAX

III   I

70. DINAH WON'T YOU BLOW YOUR HORN

Allegretto

mf

71. MOCKINGBIRD

Alice Hawthorne (Septimus Winner) (1827–1902)

Moderato

mf

p

f

72. RHYTHM RAP

Shadow bow and count before playing.

Count: 1 & a 2 & 1 & a 2 & 1 & a 2 & a 1 & 2 &

73. BLUEBERRY PIE

74. TECHNIQUE TRAX

III   I

75. RHYTHM RAP

Shadow bow and count before playing.

Count: 1 e & 2 e & 1 & 2 & 1 e & 2 e & 1 & 2 &

76. MARCHING ALONG

77. ON THE MOVE

III   I

78. RHYTHM ETUDE – Duet

A

B

79. ESSENTIAL ELEMENTS QUIZ – RHYTHM ROUND-UP

RHYTHMS

80. RHYTHM RAP

Shadow bow and count before playing.

Count: **1** e **&** a **2** e **&** a **1** **&** **2** **&** **1** e **&** a **2** e **&** a **1** **&** **2** **&**

81. TECHNIQUE TRAX

82. HOOKED ON D MAJOR

83. THE MOUNTAIN CLIMBER

84. KEEP IT SHORT

85. ESSENTIAL CREATIVITY

Write a D Major scale using any of the following rhythms: ♪♫, ♪♫, ♫♪, ♪.♪ *Perform your composition for the class.*

Syncopation

Syncopation occurs when an accent or emphasis is given to a note that is not on a strong beat. This type of "off-beat" feel is common in many popular and classical styles.

86. RHYTHM RAP

Shadow bow and count before playing.

Count: **1** & **2** & **1** & **2** & **1** & **2** & **1** & **2** &

87. SYNCOPATION TIME

88. MIRROR IMAGE

89. CHILDREN'S SHOES

Black American Spiritual

90. HOOKED ON SYNCOPATION

91. ESSENTIAL ELEMENTS QUIZ – TOM DOOLEY

American Folk Song

HALF POSITION ON THE A STRING

B♭ is played with 1 finger on the A string in half position (1/2).

Listening Skills

Play what your teacher plays. Listen carefully.

92. LET'S READ "B♭" (B-flat)

93. ROLLING ALONG

Moderato

94. MATCHING OCTAVES

HALF POSITION ON THE E STRING

F is played with 1 finger on the E string in half position (1/2).

Listening Skills

Play what your teacher plays. Listen carefully.

95. LET'S READ "F" (F-natural)

96. TECHNIQUE TRAX

THEORY

Key Signature F MAJOR

Play all B's as B♭ (B-flat).

97. F MAJOR SCALE

Half position on D string

HISTORY

A **Concerto** is a composition in several movements for solo instrument and orchestra. Exercise 98 is the theme from the first movement of the *Concerto for Violin and Orchestra* by **Ludwig van Beethoven**, composed while author William Wordsworth was writing his poem *I Wandered Lonely as a Cloud*. A special feature of the concerto is the *cadenza*, which was improvised, or made up, by the soloist during a concert. Improvising and creating your own music is great fun. Try it if you have not already.

98. THEME FROM VIOLIN CONCERTO

Ludwig van Beethoven (1770–1827)

Andante

FLAT KEYS

E♭

is played with
1 finger on the
D string in half
position (1/2).

Listening Skills   Play what your teacher plays. Listen carefully.

99. LET'S READ "E♭" (E-flat)

100. HOT CROSS BUNS

B♭

is played with
4 fingers on the
G string in half
position (1/2).

Listening Skills   Play what your teacher plays. Listen carefully.

101. LET'S READ "B♭" (B-flat)

102. VIKING WAY

103. HIKING ALONG

Key Signature
B♭ MAJOR   Play all B's as B♭ (B-flat) and all E's as E♭ (E-flat).

104. B♭ MAJOR SCALE

105. SLOVAKIAN FOLK SONG

Allegro

106. CAVALIER COUNTRY

107. ESSENTIAL ELEMENTS QUIZ – AYN KAYLOKAYNU

Andantino

Traditional Jewish Song

rit.

a tempo

△ *Return to original tempo*

FLAT KEYS

Special Double Bass Exercise

While the violins and violas are learning new notes, match the following words with the correct definitions.
Write the correct letter of the definition in the blank next to the words.

1. _____ Staccato
2. _____ Allegro
3. _____ Slur
4. _____ Intonation
5. _____ Mezzo Forte
6. _____ Interval
7. _____ Crescendo
8. _____ Moderato
9. _____ Ritardando
10. _____ Allegretto
11. _____ Legato
12. _____ Fermata
13. _____ Decrescendo
14. _____ Lento
15. _____ Andante
16. _____ Tie
17. _____ Mezzo Piano
18. _____ Forte

A. Gradually increase volume
B. Hold the note (or rest) longer
C. Curved line that connects two or more different pitches
D. Play with a stopped bow stroke
E. Slower walking tempo
F. Moderately loud
G. Gradually slow the tempo
H. Play in a smooth and connected style
I. Fast tempo
J. Moderately soft
K. Curved line that connects notes of the same pitch
L. Medium tempo
M. Lively tempo, faster than Andante, but slower then Allegro
N. How well each note is played in tune
O. A very slow tempo
P. The distance between two notes
Q. Gradually decrease volume
R. Loud

108. LET'S READ "E♭" (E-flat) – Review

109. TECHNIQUE TRAX

110. LET'S READ "B♭" (B-flat) – Review

111. TECHNIQUE BUILDER

112. B♭ MAJOR SCALE

113. THE MOUNTAIN DEER CHASE

Allegretto

North American Folk Song

114. ESSENTIAL CREATIVITY – RAKES OF MALLOW

Allegro

Irish Folk Song

Music can be created and arranged by changing rhythms and notes to an existing example. Create your own arrangement of *Rakes of Mallow* by changing the rhythms and melodic phrases. Perform your arrangement for others.

Example 1: Changing rhythms   *Example 2: Changing melodic phrases*

6/8 RHYTHMS

$\frac{6}{8}$ Time Signature

= **6 beats** per measure	♪ = 1 beat ♩ = 2 beats
= **Eighth** note gets one beat	♩. = 3 beats ♩. = 6 beats

6/8 time is usually played with a slight emphasis on the **1st** and **4th** beats of each measure.
This divides the measure into 2 groups of 3 beats each.

115. RHYTHM RAP
Shadow bow and count before playing.

116. LAZY DAY

117. HOOKED ON 6/8

Musical Form

A round is a **musical form** where performers play or sing the same melody, entering at different times. This is called counterpoint, a type of harmony. Try memorizing this round and performing it with a friend.

118. ROW, ROW, ROW YOUR BOAT – Round

American Folk Round

119. SLURRING IN 6/8 TIME

120. JOLLY GOOD FELLOW

$\begin{smallmatrix}6\\8\end{smallmatrix}$ Time Signature

When music in $\begin{smallmatrix}6\\8\end{smallmatrix}$ time is played fast, it is easier to stress beats one and four, and "feel" the pulse in two large beats.

Counted in 6 = **1** 2 3 **4** 5 6
Counted in 2 = **1** & a **2** & a

THEORY

121. RHYTHM RAP

Shadow bow and count before playing.

Count: **1** & a **2** & a   **1** & a **2** & a   **1** & a **2** & a   **1** & a **2** & a

122. RISE AND FALL

1 & a **2** & a   **1** & a **2** & a   **1** & a **2** & a   **1** & a **2** & a

123. BEACH WALK

Write in the correct time signature before you begin.

Austrian composer **Wolfgang Amadeus Mozart** was a child prodigy who lived during the American Revolution. At five, he was composing music, and by his early teens he had mastered the violin. Mozart wrote more than 600 compositions during his short life, including oratorios, symphonies, concertos, and operas.

124. MAY TIME

W. A. Mozart (1756–1791)

Allegretto

THEORY

Minor Scales

A minor scale is a series of eight notes which follow a definite pattern of whole steps and half steps. There are three forms of the minor scale; natural minor, harmonic minor, and melodic minor. The D minor (natural) scale uses the same pitches as the F major scale.

125. D MINOR (Natural) SCALE

HISTORY

Austrian composer **Gustav Mahler** was also a successful conductor. He believed in unifying the arts and often combined music, poetry, and philosophy in his compositions. Exercise 126 *Mahler's Theme* first appears in his *Symphony No. 1*, played as a solo by the double bass. During Mahler's lifetime Vincent van Gogh created his most famous paintings, and Mark Twain wrote *Tom Sawyer*.

126. MAHLER'S THEME – Round

Gustav Mahler (1860–1911)

127. SHALOM CHAVERIM – Round

Hebrew Folk Song

128. THE SNAKE CHARMER

Key Signature
G MINOR

The G minor (natural) scale uses the same pitches as the B♭ major scale.

129. G MINOR (Natural) SCALE

With the establishment of Israel as an independent political state in 1948, *Hatikvah* became the Israeli National Anthem. The same year Mohandas Gandhi was assassinated in India. Israeli violinists Itzhak Perlman and Pinchas Zukerman are concert artists known throughout the world.

130. HATIKVAH

Moderato

Israeli National Anthem

131. G MINOR (Natural) SCALE *(Upper Octave – violin)*

132. ESSENTIAL ELEMENTS QUIZ – THE HANUKKAH SONG

Allegro

Israeli Folk Song

Mixed Meter

Occasionally the meter (time signature) changes in music. Watch for meter changes and count carefully.

MIXED METER

133. RHYTHM RAP

Shadow bow and count before playing.

Count: **1** & **2** & **3** & **4** & **1** & **2** & **3** & **4** & **1** & **2** & **3** & **1** & **2** & **3** &

134. FRENCH FOLK SONG

Moderato

Cantabile

In a singing style.

e   The Italian word for "and."

135. KUM BA YAH

Andante e cantabile

African Spiritual

Triplets

A **triplet** is a group of three notes. In $\frac{2}{4}$, $\frac{3}{4}$, or $\frac{4}{4}$ time, an eighth note triplet is spread evenly across one beat.

THEORY

---

136. RHYTHM RAP

Shadow bow and count before playing.

Count: **1** **2 trip-let 3** 4 1 **2 trip-let 3** 4 **1 trip-let 2** **3 trip-let 4** **1 trip-let 2 trip-let 3** 4

---

137. D MAJOR SCALE WITH TRIPLETS

---

138. ON THE MOVE

---

139. SLURRING TRIPLETS

---

140. TRIPLET ETUDE

---

141. LITTLE RIVER

---

142. FIELD SONG

Moderato

Southern American Folk Song

f

RHYTHMS

149. RHYTHM RAP

Shadow bow and count before playing.

Count: **1** & a **2** & a **1** e & a **2** & **1** e & **2** e & **1** & **2** &

150. DOWN HOME

151. MOVING ALONG

152. RHYTHM RAP

Shadow bow and count before playing.

Count: **1** & a **2** e & **1** & **2** e & a **1** & a **2** e & **1** & **2** &

153. UP TOWN

154. FLYING BOWS

Cantatas are pieces much like short operas that were written during the **Baroque Period** (1600–1750). They involve vocal soloists and choirs that are accompanied by small orchestras. **Johann Sebastian Bach** wrote nearly 300 of them between 1704 and 1745. While Bach was composing his cantatas, the famous philosopher Voltaire was writing his books and Thomas Jefferson, the great United States president, was born.

155. MARCH FROM PEASANT'S CANTATA

Allegretto

J. S. Bach (1685–1750)

PERFORMANCE SPOTLIGHT

Performing music for others is fun and rewarding. Either small or large ensembles can perform the following arrangements. Always observe proper concert etiquette by being well prepared, dressing appropriately, being on time, and remembering all equipment. Show respect when others are playing by listening attentively and applauding at the appropriate time.

156. SAGEBRUSH OVERTURE – Orchestra Arrangement   A = Melody part. B = Orchestra part.

Arr. John Higgins

What were the strong points of your performance?

157. POMP AND CIRCUMSTANCE – Orchestra Arrangement

A = Melody part. B = Orchestra part.

Edward Elgar (1857–1933)
Arr. John Higgins

158. AMERICA THE BEAUTIFUL – Orchestra Arrangement

A = Melody part. B = Orchestra part.

Samuel Augustus Ward (1847–1903)
Arr. John Higgins

159. LA BAMBA – Duet

Mexican Folk Song
Arr. Michael Allen

PERFORMANCE SPOTLIGHT

HISTORY

Gustav Holst was a famous British orchestra composer who frequently set words to music, including poems by the American poet, Walt Whitman. Holst's *St. Paul's Suite* for string orchestra was written for the St. Paul's Girls School Orchestra and published in 1913. His best known work is *The Planets*, first performed in 1918, the same year as the end of World War I.

160. IN THE BLEAK MIDWINTER – Orchestra Arrangement

A = Melody part. **B** = Orchestra part.

Gustav Holst (1874–1934)
Arr. John Higgins

161. SWALLOWTAIL JIG – Orchestra Arrangement

Irish Jig
Arr. John Higgins

Moderately   A = Melody part. B = Orchestra part.

Sight-reading

Sight-reading means playing a musical piece for the first time. The key to sight-reading success is to know what to look for *before* you play. Use the word **S-T-A-R-S** to remind yourself what to look for, and eventually your orchestra will become sight-reading STARS!

S — **Sharps or flats** in the key signature
T — **Time signature** and **tempo markings**
A — **Accidentals** not found in the key signature
R — **Rhythms**, silently counting the more difficult notes and rests
S — **Signs**, including dynamics, articulations, repeats and endings

162. SIGHT-READING CHALLENGE #1

163. SIGHT-READING CHALLENGE #2

164. SIGHT-READING CHALLENGE #3

165. SIGHT-READING CHALLENGE #4

PREPARING FOR HIGHER POSITIONS

Natural Harmonic

Natural harmonics are tones created by a vibrating string divided into equal sections. To play an octave higher than an open string, lightly touch the string exactly half way between the bridge and the nut. In the following examples, harmonics are indicated by a "o" above a note, plus a fingering number. $\frac{3}{o}$ indicates a harmonic played with the third finger.

Shifting

Sliding your left hand smoothly and lightly to a new location on the fingerboard, indicated by a dash (–). Be sure your thumb moves with your hand.

FINGER PATTERNS (violin and viola)

While the violins and violas are practicing various finger patterns, you will be playing some new notes in new positions. All new positions are indicated with a ★ and shifts with a −. Remember to slide your hand smoothly and lightly to the new location. Always keep your thumb behind your second finger.

FINGER PATTERNS (By Pattern)

174. 3–4 PATTERN (violin, viola)

175. 2–3 PATTERN (violin, viola)

176. 1–2 PATTERN (violin, viola)

177. OPEN PATTERN (violin, viola)

FINGER PATTERNS (By String)

178. E STRING

179. A STRING

180. D STRING

181. G STRING

182. C STRING *(viola, cello)*

42

FINGER PATTERNS (By Key)

183. C MAJOR

184. G MAJOR

185. D MAJOR

FINGER PATTERNS

186. A MAJOR

187. F MAJOR

(viola, cello)

188. B♭ MAJOR

(viola, cello)

FINGER PATTERNS

SCALES AND ARPEGGIOS

Identify two important elements of performing scales and arpeggios accurately.
As you play each line, check to make sure you are able to do these things.

189. C MAJOR

190. C MAJOR *(Lower Octave – viola and cello)*

191. G MAJOR

192. G MAJOR *(Upper Octave – violin)*

193. D MAJOR

194. D MAJOR *(Lower Octave – viola and cello)*

195. A MAJOR

196. A MAJOR *(Upper Octave – violin)*

197. F MAJOR

198. B♭ MAJOR

199. B♭ MAJOR *(Upper Octave – violin)*

200. D MINOR (Natural)

201. D MINOR (Natural) *(Lower Octave – viola and cello)*

202. G MINOR (Natural)

203. G MINOR (Natural) *(Upper Octave – violin)*

CREATING MUSIC

THEORY

Improvisation

Improvisation is the art of freely creating your own music as you play.

204. *Using the following notes, improvise your own melody (Line A) to go with the accompaniment (Line B).*

THEORY

Composition

Composition is the art of writing original music. A composer often begins by creating a melody made up of individual **phrases**, like short musical "sentences." Some melodies have phrases that seem to answer or respond to "question" phrases, as in Beethoven's *Ode To Joy*. Play this melody and listen to how phrase 2 answers phrase 1.

205. ODE TO JOY

Ludwig van Beethoven (1770–1827)

206. PHRASE BUILDERS *Write 2 different phrases using the following rhythms.*

207. Q. AND A. *Write your own "answer" to the following melodies.*

208. YOU NAME IT: _____ *Now write your own music.*

IMPROVISATION/COMPOSITION

Double Stops

A **double stop** is playing two strings at once.

209. TWO AT A TIME

210. ADDING FINGERS

DOUBLE BASS FINGERING CHART

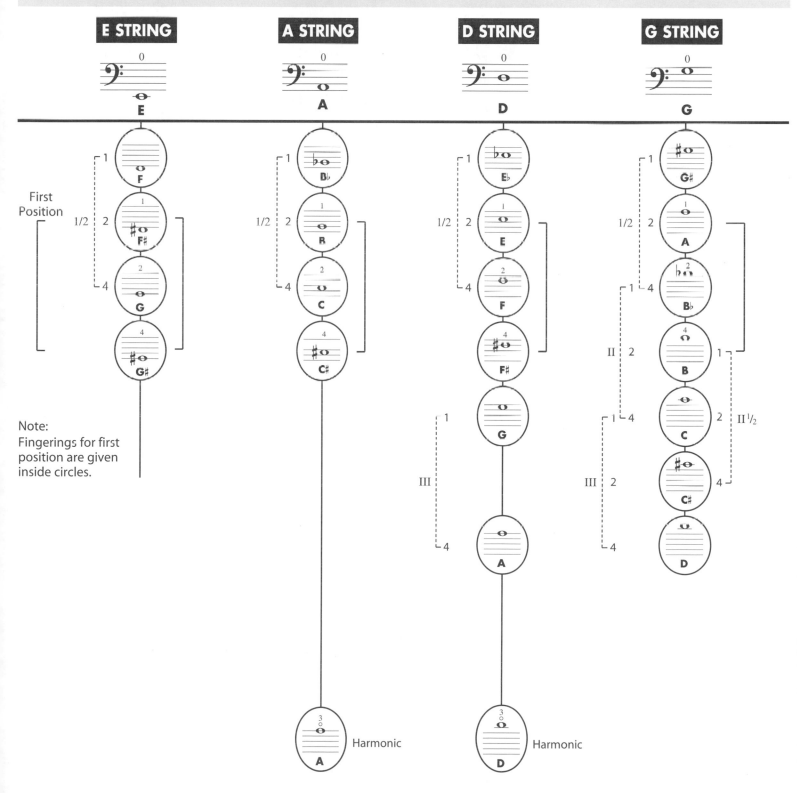

REFERENCE INDEX

Definitions (pg.)

A Tempo 23
Accent 15
Alle Breve 32
Allegretto 6
Andantino 11
Cantabile 30
Cantata 33
Composition 46
Concerto 21
Crescendo *(cresc.)* 3
Cut Time 32
Decrescendo *(decresc.)* 3
Dotted Quarter Note 10
Double Stop 47
Dynamics 3, 7
e 30
Eighth rest 9
Fermata 10
Finger Patterns 40 *(violin & viola)*
Harmonic 39
Improvisation 46
Interval 4
Intonation 5
Legato 2
Lento 11
Meter Change 30
Mezzo piano (*mp*) 7
Mezzo forte (*mf*) 7
Minor Scale 28
Ritardando *(rit.)* 11
Round 26
Sight-reading 38
6/8 26
Sixteenth Notes 16
Shifting 39
Syncopation 19
Triplet 31

Book I Review

Allegro 5
Andante 4
Bow Lift 3
Common Time 7
Dotted Half Note 3
Eighth Note 3
1st & 2nd Endings 3
Forte (*f*) 3

Half Note 2
Hooked Bowing 4
Major Scale 2
Moderato 3
Piano (*p*) 3
Quarter Note 2
Slur 2
Staccato 6
Tie 3
Tone 7
Whole Note 2

Composers

J.S. BACH
• March from "Peasant's Cantata" 33

LUDWIG VAN BEETHOVEN
• Theme from "Violin Concerto in D" 21
• Ode To Joy 46

WILLIAM BILLINGS
• Chester 4

ANTONIN DVOŘÁK
• Theme from "New World Symphony" 11

EDWARD ELGAR
• Pomp and Circumstance 35

STEPHEN COLLINS FOSTER
• Oh! Susannah 8

EDVARD GRIEG
• Morning from "Peer Gynt" 3

ALICE HAWTHORNE (SEPTIMUS WINNER)
• Mockingbird 16

FRANZ JOSEPH HAYDN
• Theme from "London Symphony" 2

GUSTAV HOLST
• In the Bleak Midwinter 36

GUSTAV MAHLER
• Theme from "Symphony No. 1" 28

JEAN-JOSEPH MOURET
• Rondeau 11

WOLFGANG AMADEUS MOZART
• May Time 27

JACQUES OFFENBACH
• Barcarolle 3

HENRY PURCELL
• Rigaudon 8

SAMUEL WARD
• America The Beautiful 35

COOL WHITE (JOHN HODGES)
• Buffalo Gals 6

World Music

AFRICAN
• Kum Bah Yah 30

AMERICAN
• America The Beautiful 35
• A Capital Ship 11
• Children's Shoes 19
• Mountain Deer Chase 25
• Field Song 31
• Jesse James 9
• The Streets of Laredo 34
• Tom Dooley 19
• Row, Row, Row Your Boat 26
• When The Saints Go Marching In 32
• Yellow Rose of Texas 34

ENGLISH
• Jolly Good Fellow 26

FRENCH
• At Pierrot's Door 12
• Alouette 8
• French Folk Song 30

HEBREW/ ISRAELI
• Ayn Kaylokaynu 23
• The Hannukah Song 29
• Hatikvah 29
• Shalom Chaverim 28

IRISH
• Rakes of Mallow 25
• Swallowtail Jig 37

MEXICAN
• La Bamba 36

RUSSIAN
• Russian Folk Tune 14
• Sitka City 15

SLOVAKIA
• Slovakian Folk Song 23